# BOOTS TO BOGIES TO BRONZE

The authorized World War II biography
of 2Lt. Jack C. Pyatt

By Martin Capages Jr. Ph.D.

Map Courtesy of the 13th Armored Division

© 2018 Martin Capages, Jr.

All rights reserved. No part of this book may be reproduced or utilized in any form or by any means, electronic or mechanical, including photocopying, recording or by any information storage retrieval system without permission in writing from the publisher, except for a reviewer who may quote brief passages in a review to be printed in a newspaper, magazine or electronic publication.

**American Freedom Publications LLC**

www.americanfreedompublications.com

2638 E. Wildwood Road

Springfield, Missouri 65804

ISBN 978-1-64255-956-9   Paperback Version

**Cover Design**   American Freedom Publications LLC

**Manuscript Editor**   American Freedom Publications LLC

First Edition- January 20, 2018

Printed in the United States of America

## DEDICATION

This biography was authorized by Jack Conrad Pyatt and is dedicated to the heroes of the 13th Armored Division "Black Cats" and the Second Calvary Division.

## ACKNOWLEDGEMENTS

I want to thank Patty Bellamy, daughter of Frank Bellamy 46th Tank Battalion, for her contribution and persistence in the development of the 13th Armored Division website and her publication of the first edition of *Boots to Bogies to Bronze* on that website.

I also want to acknowledge the source of the summarized histories of these fighting units, The Second Calvary and the 13th Armored Divisions published by the Army & Navy Publishing Company of Baton Rouge, Louisiana in 1941 and 1946 respectively.

Many of the photographs in this biography were personal photos taken by Jack Pyatt which were also included in the Army & Navy Publishing Company's unit yearbooks. Other photographs, taken by military personnel or their immediate families and posted on the 13th Armored Division website, were included as appropriate. Any WWII Second Calvary or 13th Armored Division veteran who desires a copy of *Boots to Bogies to Bronze* may have one for the cost of printing and shipping only by accessing the email contact page on the American Freedom Publications LLC website, [www.americanfreedompublications.com](www.americanfreedompublications.com).

## TABLE OF CONTENTS

DEDICATION ..................................................................... iii
ACKNOWLEDGEMENTS ..................................................... iv
PREFACE ......................................................................... vii
The Second Calvary Division ............................................. 1
The 8th Armored Division ................................................. 5
The 13th Armored Division ............................................... 7
FRANCE ......................................................................... 14
    LE HAVRE ................................................................. 14
    SOISSON .................................................................. 17
    CHAZELLES .............................................................. 17
    ST. GOAR ................................................................. 18
GERMANY ...................................................................... 21
    ALTENKIRCHEN ........................................................ 21
    SIEGBURG ............................................................... 23
    WAHNERHEIDE AND MULHEIM ................................ 23
    DUNNWALD ............................................................ 25
    EHRBACH ................................................................ 27
    DELLBRUCK ............................................................. 30
    SEELSCHEID ............................................................ 32
    METTMAN .............................................................. 36
    OPLADEN ................................................................ 38
    DUISBERG ............................................................... 39
AUSTRIA ........................................................................ 43
    LINZ ........................................................................ 43
    NEU OTTING ........................................................... 50
    EGGENFELDEN ........................................................ 52
EPILOGUE ...................................................................... 59
ABOUT THE AUTHOR ...................................................... 62
References ..................................................................... 64
INDEX ............................................................................ 65

## PREFACE

This is the war story of a quiet, distinguished gentleman who once lived in my neighborhood named Jack Pyatt. Jack lived in a well-groomed home on a circular drive in Wildwood Estates in southeast Greene County, Missouri. I had met Jack several years ago and we became good friends even though he was a generation ahead of me. You see, Jack Pyatt served in the US Army during World War II. So did my dad, but my dad was a US Marine lieutenant who served in the Pacific Theater and fought against the Japanese in Okinawa while Jack fought in the European Theater against the Germans. Like most WWII vets, both men would not talk about their experience, you had to literally pull it out of them. My dad passed away in May 1997 at age 78. I regret that I did not learn much about Dad's wartime experience. While Jack would leave us at age 92 on April 1, 2011, I wasn't going to miss the opportunity to hear his story.

About fifteen years ago, I invited Jack to go sailing with me on Table Rock Lake. I needed some help handling my sailboat, the Derringer, in a race and so, I recruited Jack to help crew the boat. I also recruited my brother-in-law Jack Myer to help crew the boat. That was a mistake. While both men were quite capable, they were both named Jack. After several miscues, we decided they would respond to their last names when following instructions.

**Jack Pyatt on the Derringer**

At that time, I didn't know much about Jack Pyatt's World War II experience. But, I'll never forget the story he told as I coerced him to talk about his service <u>one line at a time</u>. I met with Jack several times after that and convinced him to tell me his story again, so I could write it down.

**The Derringer Underway**

This biography is the result of that effort to document the World War II experience of this quiet, somewhat shy, unpretentious American hero. We would meet together several times to put together his story. As dementia started to set in, Jack would repeat several of his wartime episodes. The stories never wavered.

It was my pleasure to escort Jack to an interview with a group of people who were in the process of memorializing these WWII veterans by recording their stories. During that interview, Jack showed the interviewers his copy of the First Edition of his biography. One young boy asked if he could have a signed copy of the biography. Jack signed it and gave it to the young fellow. Later on, Jack received a copy of the interview on a DVD and we watched the interview together. I will never forget his comments about the war. According to Jack, "We were not ready, but we got ready fast!"

The first edition of this biography was submitted to the 13th Armored Division website at www.13tharmoreddivision.org prior to Jack's passing and has been available for viewing since 2008. This publication is an update of that first Edition.

Martin Capages, Jr. PhD

## THE SECOND CALVARY DIVISION

Jack Pyatt left Webster Groves, Missouri and began his military experience as a draftee in the horse cavalry at Fort Riley, Kansas in the spring of 1941, before the Japanese attack at Pearl Harbor on December 7, 1941. At that time the Army had from 6 to 10 thousand horses, called remounts, ready for combat service. Fort Riley was the home of the newly organized Second Calvary Division. This Division can trace its lineage back to the early part of the 19th century and was composed of a group of the oldest cavalry regiments in the United States Army. The unit was activated on April 1, 1941.

The 2$^{nd}$ Cavalry Division was stationed at Camp Funston, Fort Riley, Kansas. While Camp Funston was used for housing troops during World War I, after the war, this once active camp had fallen back into its original state

**Corporal Jack C Pyatt**

called Funston's Pastures. With the beginning of the Defense Program just before we entered World War II, work was launched in such great haste that buildings were begun at the rate of one every 45 minutes and every 39 minutes a new structure was completed. The training of raw recruits was rigorous since most of those from Selective Service had never ridden a horse. The training was designed to build raw material into competent horsemen skilled in the use of arms. Jack was a Corporal in Battery B of the Third Field Artillery Battalion of the 2nd Calvary Division.

**Battery B, Third Field Artillery Battalion, 2nd Calvary Division**

Jack Pyatt and Tom Thumb

While the training was intensive, he still enjoyed his tour of duty in Kansas and loved jumping a trio of his favorite steeds, Tom Thumb, Oscar, and Variety. He was promoted to Corporal then Staff Sergeant in rapid order.

Pyatt Jumping Tom Thumb

2nd Calvary on Maneuvers in Kansas

In 1936, the ways to wage war changed. The Germans had developed mechanized warfare and successfully implemented "blitzkrieg" (lightning war) by invading Poland in 1939. The end of the days of the horse-mounted soldier were evident in the movie news films of the Polish cavalry in retreat before the onslaught of the air supported mechanized German Wehrmacht. At Fort Riley, Kansas things changed. The role of horses pulling artillery caissons was over. <u>The horse soldiers were out of a job.</u>

**German Panzer and Infantry**

**German Stuka Dive Bombers**

## THE 8ᵀᴴ ARMORED DIVISION

Staff Sergeant Jack Pyatt was transferred to Fort Knox, Kentucky where he was assigned to training members of the medical corps on close order drill, digging latrines, and how to stay alive in combat. After weeks of what he considered to be a misuse of combat resources, Sergeant Pyatt wrote a letter of complaint to the commanding general. In the letter he said, "This is a complete waste of good combat troops". <u>Unfortunately, he didn't go through the chain of command.</u>

A colonel came to see him and advised him that he was in a "load of trouble". The colonel escorted him to the commanding general where Jack expected the worst, maybe even some time in the Brig. The general was sitting behind a large desk

**Training 8th Armored Medics**

**A Field Combat Carry**

with Jack's personnel folder in front of him. He looked up at Jack with a scowl on his face and growled, "Sergeant Pyatt, do you know anything about the Army chain of command?". After a dressing down by the general, the general came around from behind his desk and escorted Jack to the door. "Dismissed", he said. Jack snapped a salute and started out the door. The general swatted him on the fanny with the personnel file and said, "get out of here", then winked.

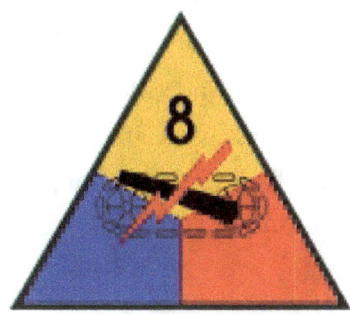

Jack was officially transferred to the 8th Armored Division. The 8th Armored Division had been activated at Fort Knox, Kentucky, on 1 April 1942. The Division was initially called the 'Iron Snake', but subsequently adopted the 'Thundering Herd' moniker and another, it's war code name of 'Tornado'. From June 1942 until January 1943 it served as a training division. It trained cadre and replacements for many other armored divisions. While stationed at Fort Knox, the Division was the official military guardian of the United States Gold Vault.

Jack was a member of the training cadre and would be promoted to First Sergeant and transferred to the 13th Armored Division at Camp Beale, California. Just like Fort Knox, there would be no horses there either. <u>His new saddle was going to be made of steel.</u>

## THE 13TH ARMORED DIVISION

First Sergeant Jack Pyatt joined the 13th Armored Division. The 13th Armored, known as the Black Cats, was 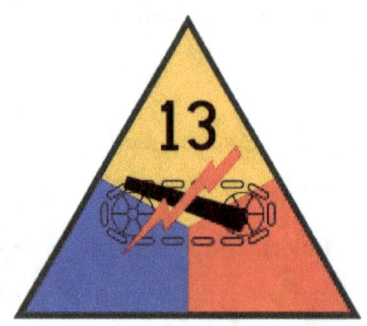 activated on 15 October 1942 at Camp Beale, California, East of Marysville. From activation day until the end of the year, fillers (both officers and enlisted men) continued to arrive, until the Division was at full strength. During this period, the training concentrated on maintenance of vehicles, short road marches, small arms training, and the shifting of personnel within the battalion to put the right men in the right spot.

**A-Company 24th Tank Battalion at Camp Beal, California**
First Sergeant Jack Pyatt in Center of First Row

As First Sergeant of Company A, Jack Pyatt had his hands full. Most of the work of any Army company is accomplished by the non-commissioned officers and the First Sergeant has overall responsibility for the performance of the unit, that's why the nickname for First Sergeant is "Top".

**13th Armored Training at Camp Beale, California**

In October, the battalion participated in the Division's birthday celebration, and later spent a week at Camp Kohler, near Sacramento, where small arms ranges allowed for concentrated training on this subject for a few days. November brought an inspection of the

**Getting Ready**

division by officers from the Armored Command Headquarters, and the battalion began to realize that inspections would be hounding them for the rest of their Army careers.

Early in December, orders were received for a change of station to Camp Bowie, Texas, and the whole Division loaded aboard trains and proceeded there. Camp Bowie, they found, was close to Brownwood, Texas a small town some 100 miles from Fort Worth. As a training area, it was fine. The camp itself was in one corner of the reservation, and the reservation was large enough for the Division to operate firing ranges and have field problems simultaneously, which had been almost impossible to do at Camp Beale. As a place to live, however, it had its limitations. Brownwood itself was too small to furnish living accommodations for all those who wanted to live there, and amusement for all who wanted to amuse themselves there. Fort Worth and Dallas were a long distance away, and transportation there and back was difficult to get and expensive when we got it. It was too wet and cold in the winter, and too hot and dry in the summer.

The year 1944 was full of rumors. "We were going to Knox. We were going back to Beale. We were going to Africa. We were going to England. We were going to the Pacific. We weren't going anywhere." Nobody knew. What they did was stay at Camp Bowie. In January the

Division took the I.T.P. tests again, to show the new Corps commander that they still remembered their individual training. Early in February, the battalion went on what is called the 'D' Series, consisting of three weeks of field problems, during which time no one returned to the camp comforts. "It was during this series that we convinced ourselves that we had learned to live in the field." The weather was atrocious – cold, windy and wet. "The hours were long and we didn't get much sleep. We got wet and muddy, and couldn't get dry for a long time. But sick call went down, and the colds, which had been many in camp, almost disappeared. When we came back to camp near the end of February, we were convinced that we had that part of the art of war licked."

March, April and May were spent in more training. Ammunition was easier to obtain, and the tank and artillery battalions did a great deal of firing out in the artillery area on the south and east sides of the reservation. June brought an inspection by General McNair, Commanding General of the Army Ground Forces.

In July, the Division spent three days on maneuvers with the 12th Armored Division, which came to Bowie to take their Division Test. Early in October, the Division put on a demonstration of the assault of a heavily fortified area which brought into play all elements of the Division, as well as a squadron of fighter-bombers from a nearby air base.

Live ammunition was used throughout the attack, which was conducted over ground and against fortifications similar to the Siegfried Line in Germany.

During the whole period at Camp Bowie, inspections were frequent – almost continuous, in fact. But beginning in October, the heat really started to get put on. In November, packing instruction took priority in our training, and in the middle of December, the men were given the final War Department inspection which was given to all units just before going overseas. After three years of teaching tank tactics as a member of the armored training cadre, Jack went with the 13$^{th}$ Armored Division, 24$^{th}$ Tank Battalion to the European Theater.

According to Jack, "Things began to happen as soon as we climbed on that train to leave Bowie January 4, 1945 and kept right on happening. The Division rolled into the staging area at Camp Kilmer, New Jersey on 8 January and began processing, checking records and clothing, and training, and visited New York for a last quick handshake with civilization before embarking. About the first thing we remember after that fling in New York was staggering up the gangplank of the troop transport ship, Exceller. Some of the other units were boarding the Sea Quail. I think there were over twenty transports.

We wandered through a maze of hatches, companionways, ladders and ended up at little bunks. The enlisted trooper bunks were so close together, one above the other that the troopers almost had to breathe in cadence. I was lucky and had been assigned to the non-commissioned officer's area where we had a bit more room. I remember talking with my fellow non-coms and one guy blurted out that he was craving some type of pie, any pie. Well, one of our group, I believe his nickname was Hay-Jac, overheard this comment and swiped a pie from the cooks in the galley when they weren't looking. The pie was still hot, and he hid it under his shirt against his belly. He managed to get it up to our quarters but when he produced the pie it had burned his stomach and the look of the pie was not very appetizing."

The Exceller seemed pretty big to Sergeant Pyatt and his platoon members at first, sitting there in the calm harbor. But it appeared to shrink as the ship plunged through the Atlantic. The trip across was made as part of a huge convoy which assembled some distance offshore, and included the British battleship H.M.S. 'Nelson' cruising alongside the convoy all the way across. In the main, the ocean voyage was made without incident. One of the ships broke down and had to return to New York, the convoy was twice alerted for submarines and depth charges were dropped. Most of the troop passengers were afflicted with seasickness. On January 28 the ship anchored off Southampton, England, to wait for a high tide before running across the English Channel to a French port. "We thought about how easy it was for us compared to those who went before us on D-day last June. Thanks to those brothers-in-arms, we would face no resistance and would land in France like a bunch of tourists".

**The HMS Nelson**

## FRANCE

LE HAVRE

The men of the 13th Division were in good shape when the troopships reached the devastated port that had been Le Havre, France on 29 January 1945. The morning of the 29th they got their first glimpse of France when the ship tied up at Le Havre docks. Shattered piers and buildings testified to the terrific bombing the city had undergone. The French people were, ragged and dirty, scrambling along the dock and even into the water for the cigarettes, candy bars and oranges they tossed down to them. The once sunny French countryside was bleak and frozen under the worst snow storm in many years. The French railroad still pulled boxcars labeled 4O Hommes & 8 Chevaux but they must have been cleaner in World War I. [The label in World War I was actually *Quarante Hommes ou Huit Chevaux* (Forty Men or Eight Horses)] We rode them to St. Ouen de Breuil, then moved in trucks to Bellencombre, St. Hellier, and Rosay. Here in apple-rich Normandy, the men of the 13th Armored Division "Black Cats" would sharpen their claws for two months in preparation for battle.

Sergeant Pyatt was still assigned as First Sergeant in Company A of the 24th Tank Battalion, a part of Combat

Command 'B' of the overall Combat Command. The Combat Command comprised approximately one third of the 13$^{th}$ Division's fighting strength - one of its three battle groups. It was composed of the Combat Command B Headquarters and Headquarters Company, 59$^{th}$ Armored Infantry Battalion, 24$^{th}$ Tank Battalion, 496$^{th}$ Armored Field Artillery Battalion, Company B of the 124$^{th}$ Armored Engineer Battalion, Company A of the 83$^{rd}$ Medical Battalion, Company A of the 135$^{th}$ Ordnance Maintenance Battalion and Troop B of the 93$^{rd}$ Cavalry Reconnaissance Squadron (Mechanized). (13th Armored Division, 24th Tank Battalion, 1946)

BELLENCOMBRE

The various units were billeted in all sorts of buildings, ranging from magnificent 17$^{th}$ century chateaus to dilapidated barns. The armor and weapons of war began to roll in and the troops busied themselves unpacking equipment, removing Cosmoline from arms, stripping vehicles of wax, mounting radios, checking tracks and bogies, building carriage racks, and fulfilling the various details necessary for armored divisions in combat.

**Waiting in Bellencombre**

For some of the newer troops the preparation included sewing on a familiar little triangular, yellow, red and blue patch - the $13^{th}$ Armored Division sleeve insignia.

On the evening of March 15, the GI's made their last rounds of the social establishments in their respective little French villages before loading up in tanks, half-tracks, armored cars, jeeps and trucks. At 2200 hours that evening unit commanders gave their orders; the columns started to roll, and the march across France was underway. Combat Command 'A', Combat Command 'B' and Division Artillery, the Division, moved by night and day. It followed a route across the northern part of France; through historic Compiegne, where the treaty of 1918 was signed and where Hitler forced reversal of procedure in 1940; and through Chateau-Thierry.

## SOISSON

The first eight-hour stopover for rest and maintenance was made in Soisson, a city liberated by a sister armored division. After a meal, refueling and forty winks, the column was back on the road. Riding all night, Vitry-le-Francios was reached in the morning where a repetition of the Soisson halt was made. Fortunate elements of the division passed through Nancy in day-light, and saw the largest city yet observed by troops of the $13^{th}$, with the exception of a few lucky members who had managed to get to Paris. Finally, the column closed in on their bivouac areas in the vicinity of Avricourt, where Division Headquarters was set up. The Division Artillery pulled out on 19 March to become the first of the $13^{th}$ Division troops committed to the fight, pouring shells into the besieged city of Saarbruken. "A" Battery of the $497^{th}$ dropped in the first shell from Spicheren, Germany.

## CHAZELLES

The Division got under way again March 25 and Combat Command 'B', established a command post in Chateau de Gd Seilles in the vicinity of Chazelles, France.

On 26 March orders were received for the Combat Command to march to an assembly area in the vicinity of Zweibrucken, Germany with the mission of policing and supporting Military Government there. Easter Sunday, April 1, brought close to one hundred percent of the soldiers throughout the entire division out to attend Easter Services with their respective units. The following day the Combat Command was ordered to the vicinity of Kirn, Germany for further duties as occupational troops. During the period of April 2-4, inclusive, the main efforts of the Combat Command were directed towards traffic control in support of Military Government along with personal and vehicular maintenance. At that time the Combat Command's S-3, along with G-3 of Division, was at Frankfurt a Main receiving orders for the Combat Command to displace to the vicinity of Alsfeld, Germany. The 13th Armored Division, attached to the VIII Corps, had been given the mission of relieving the veteran 4th Armored Division in the vicinity of Eisenach, Germany.

ST. GOAR

At 1300 hours on 5 April, the column rolled across the pontoon bridge at St. Goar, crossing the Europe's largest river, the Rhine. General Patton, Third U.S. Army

Commander, then assigned the 13<sup>th</sup> to XX Corps. The mission however, remained the same. The following day the Combat Command moved from Alsfeld to the vicinity of Melsungen, Germany, for two days in which maintenance and re-supply in preparation for combat. In route overhead the ever-welcome P-51s and P38s rode herd over the earthbound vehicles.

On 8 April the Division received orders to relieve the 4<sup>th</sup> Armored and directing it on an important mission in the Ruhr Valley. Attached to the XVIII Corps (Airborne), the Division was now part of the First Army. In the rapid advance of the First and Ninth U.S. Armies into the interior of Germany, they by-passed an area of approximately 400 square miles, bordered on the South by the Sieg River and moving West along the Sieg to the Rhine; North along the Rhine to the outskirts of Cologne and on up into the industrial area of Essen and Dortmund. The 13<sup>th</sup> Armored Division was given the task of spearheading the attack upon the Ruhr from the South.

**Crossing the Rhine at St. Goar**

**GERMANY**

ALTENKIRCHEN

**The Crossing of Sieg River**

The next move was to march the Division to the vicinity of Altenkirchen, Germany, to take up position and prepare for the jump-off across the Sieg River. On 8 April the $24^{th}$ Tank Battalion set out for Schonberg to join the First Army for a Ruhr Valley cleanup. This involved 159 miles of hard driving required an extended period of time for repair and maintenance of tanks and vehicles before going into action. Maintenance crews performed the impossible by delivering most of the tanks in time for the crossing of the Sieg River. Combat Command B was given instructions from Corps to cross the $97^{th}$'s bridge over the Sieg River and drive northward to the vicinity of Dunnwald then swing northeast and spearhead toward the objective in the vicinity of Huckswagen, Germany.

**COMBAT COMMAND A AND B**

The Combat Command was now broken down into two task forces, a tank task force and an infantry task force with armored support. The Tank Task Force was made up of the $24^{th}$ Tankers, minus Company A of the tankers, plus

B Company of the 59th Armored Infantry Battalion. The Infantry Task Force was composed of the 59th Armored Infantry Battalion minus Company B and plus A Company of the 24th (Jack Pyatt's Unit). Both Task Forces were ordered to reconnoiter the bridgehead and routes of approach to it on the morning of the 9 April.

**155 Self Propelled Rifle**

Surplus equipment was dropped off in Schonberg, and the 24th moved to a forward assembly just south of the Sieg River early 10 April. The Battalion first came under fire at 1000 just west of the bridge over the Agger. The leading elements of the column were subjected to light enemy artillery as they entered the city. A blown overpass in Siegburg blocked the advance temporarily, but a by-pass was established through a railroad yard by doughboys of company A. In the operation two of the infantrymen were wounded and one halftrack damaged by an enemy mortar shell.

## SIEGBURG

A circuitous route around a road block Northeast of Siegburg brought the head of the column to the Autobahn, Germany's super-highway, where the Task Force could travel at rapid rates, crushing all light opposition in the way, and soon reach the Agger River. Reaching the river the troops found the bridges blown and the stream too deep to ford. That night the unit coiled in Siegburg.

## WAHNERHEIDE AND MULHEIM

On 11 April, the Infantry Task Force, following the Tank Task Force moved into Elsdorf under light enemy artillery and mortar fire to clear two road blocks by-passed by the preceding Tank Task Force. The leading elements of the Infantry Task Force reached Vingst around sunset, but the 59th Armored Infantry Battalion Headquarters had become detached from the column when small arms fire and heavy artillery and mortar fire fell on the vehicles while passing through Rath. Reorganizing, these elements managed to move forward to rejoin the Task Force at Vingst shortly after daylight the next morning.

The Infantry Task Force moving toward Dunnwald that afternoon was ambushed after proceeding only four miles. Sniper fire commenced, then artillery fire dropped in while Company D mangled two 88 guns at Spitze. Company B moved in to smash antiaircraft guns. Company B led on through Wahnerheide, turned west into four antitank guns, flak guns and riflemen and crushed them in a half-hour fight while the battalion was reorganizing east of town. Unable to rejoin the battalion, B Company spent the night on an airfield southwest of Mulheim. Snapping into action at dawn when visibility revealed 88-mm. and flak guns ringing the field, alert assault gun crews from Headquarters Company, tanks and infantry fought their way from the trap and moved north to join the battalion west of Dunnwald shortly before noon on the 12 April.

**German 88 mm Anti-Aircraft Anti-Tank Gun**

DUNNWALD

The resistance in the small village was quickly eliminated enabling the Task Force to race rapidly to the outskirts of Dunnwald, where the column was again delayed by road blocks. An attempt to reduce these defended road blocks brought about a counter-attack from an enemy force, and bitter fighting took place. Ten men from one platoon of C Company of the 59th were killed before the counter attack was repelled while seventy-seven of the enemy were killed and 142 taken prisoner. The Task Force assembled under intermittent artillery fire at Dunnwald.

Jack Pyatt's M-4 Sherman tank variant with 90 mm Gun

At 0900 hours on 13 April, the second platoon of the Engineer Company completed the bridge across the Agger. Most of the construction was done under enemy fire. At 0930, the Tank Task Force started to roll across the bridge and overran a few under-manned enemy strong points, taking many bewildered prisoners. Particularly amazed were the captured enemy Air Corps personnel who surrendered. They hadn't been expecting the Americans to be there for another day or two.

**Unusual German Aircraft in Munich or Mulheim**

The Infantry Task Force now following up behind the Tank Task Force crashed rapidly on, meeting only sporadic resistance. B and D Companies of the 24th Tankers working in close cooperation and employing a cagey strategy knocked out two 88mm and five 40mm guns in the vicinity of Spich. The attack continued North to Wahnerheide, which was taken without a scrap, then turned west. Just outside of Wahnerheide the leading tanks of B Company hit upon an enemy strongpoint consisting of two 75mm guns and two 40mm flak guns with an unknown number of riflemen and machine guns. Fierce fighting followed with heavy bursts and tracer flashes coming from both directions. However, by the coordination of tank and artillery fire the enemy was destroyed within thirty minutes. In the fierce exchange of fire one medium tank was lost - the first Combat Command B tank to fall to the enemy.

EHRBACH

As the morning of 12 April, heavy firing was heard coming from the nearby town of Ehrbach. A reconnaissance team from B Troops of the 93rd was sent to investigate the situation. The trains of Combat Command B had been ambushed by a strong and well-organized enemy, estimated to be at least 250 men.

A Task Team was organized, consisting of by two medium tanks from A Company of the 24th (Jack Pyatt's unit) a light tank, two tank destroyers, and the 4th Platoon of Company 'A', which was attached to Headquarters, Combat Command B. The Task Team shortly obtained artillery support from the 496th. Two M7's bearing 105mm howitzers from A Battery moved to the scene and adjusted direct fire while an observer was also sent to observe indirect fire for C Battery. A very spirited engagement ensued but soon the German force, beaten by the pounding of the artillery, was forced to surrender. The 4th Platoon of Company A suffered nine casualties in the first few minutes but assisted in repelling the attack and in taking a large number of prisoners. The Transportation platoon of Service Company also took part in this action and suffered

**Flame Throwing Tank Against Pillbox**

heavily, with four drivers killed and six wounded. From prisoners captured, it was learned that the enemy was actually 350 strong. During this action the S-4 from the 496th and his crew of three enlisted men were captured but in the excitement of the battle they managed to escape and kill the officer holding them. Approximately 50 enemy were killed in the hot fighting and 250 were captured.

Late in the afternoon of the 12 April, Combat Command Headquarters and the remainder of the Combat command still in the rear, by-passed Ehrbach and joined the Combat Command at Dunnwald, where the Command Post was established for reorganization. The 496th also displaced and followed close behind the advance to the North and closed in position in the vicinity of Aus, near Dellbruck, and immediately came under 88mm fire and small arms attack. One platoon of infantry soon arrived from the 59th to take over the situation and chase the enemy from the surrounding woods. The artillery battalion remained in this position for two days while the Combat Command was regrouping for continued attack to the Northeast. All units of the Combat Command were harassed by 88mm mortar fire from the enemy in this area. It was learned from Russians, who had been slave laborers in the area for some time that German guns, which appeared to be knocked out and unmanned, were doing most of the firing on the troops of the command. The Russians pointed out the positions of several 88mm batteries to the 496th; the artillery sent out observers to check on the locations, bring fire on the German guns, and destroy them. With the aid of their aerial observation the artillery wiped out many enemy guns while in this position, including one enemy flak battery which was completely destroyed.

DELLBRUCK

Combat Command reorganized, and plans were drawn for an attack to the Northeast. With the Infantry Task Force leading off, the attack got under way on the afternoon of Friday the 13 April. The Task Force received fire from multiple enemy automatic weapon positions. Leading elements approaching Kemper were forced to by-pass a road block and in doing so were caught in Panzerfaust fire which knocked out one half-track, and automatic weapons fire so highly concentrated that a withdrawal of the leading troops was necessary. Twenty casualties were suffered in these elements.

As night approached, a defensive position was established, and artillery support was obtained. The 496th laid time fire in the area during the night. Units of the Combat Command in Dunnwald came under observed artillery fire and after suffering numerous casualties, decided to move to the road East of Dunnwald and finally coil in a field adjacent to Dellbruck.

# BRONZE STAR BATTLE ACTION

## SEELSCHEID

On 13 April, the 3$^{rd}$ tank platoon consisting of five Sherman tanks under the command of 2LT Noah Krall was ambushed by enemy forces in the small town of Seelscheid, Germany.

**Entrance to SeelSheid**

The tanks had their treads blown off and their armor penetrated with Panzerfaust. The tanks were out of action. The tank crews had abandoned their tanks and were trapped against a rock wall around a stone church building.

The group came under the withering fire of small arms and mortars with three men injured. At that time First

Sergeant Pyatt was monitoring the situation on the radio. He had to serve as First Sergeant and as the first platoon tank commander when he had to take over the platoon when the previous platoon leader, Second Lieutenant George Cantley, was shot in an earlier action. The first platoon had replaced two of its Shermans with the new Pershing tank with a 90-mm gun. The tank crews were in the process of "shaking down" the new equipment. First Sgt. Pyatt was very concerned that his platoon would wind up in the same condition as Lt. Krall's. He therefore decided to take a ¾ ton truck with a 30 caliber Browning and driver to scout out the area before committing any tank platoons to extricate the trapped 3rd platoon tanks.

**Damaged Sherman Tank of 3rd Platoon**

He found that Lt. Krall and his troops were trapped against an old rock fence on the perimeter of church yard. Sgt. Pyatt noticed that the Germans were not firing on the church, so he went back to Lt. Krall's position and told him to get his men over to the church so that artillery fire could be called in on the position. Jack and his driver loaded the wounded in the truck and lead Lt. Krall and his troopers who could still walk over to the church. Then they called in the artillery fire all around the church. This stopped the small arms and Panzerfaust immediately.

**PFC Gossett Checks Damage**

Sgt. Pyatt and his driver then returned to his unit with the wounded troopers, capturing over 20 prisoners on the way back. "They just came out of the hedgerows with their hands over their heads. It was just me, my driver and Lt. Krall's wounded tankers. We didn't have our tanks with us. The brass didn't like the idea that a non-com and a driver had done all this to save an officer and his stranded tanks. So, when they submitted the paperwork for the Bronze Star, the citation said we went in with our ¾ truck and a tank platoon. But I didn't bring my tank platoon, it was too risky".

**Company C of 45th Tank Battalion with 20 German POWs**

The Tank Task Force had been given the new objective of taking Wiehagen and in compliance with the order moved out of its position in Dunnwald. With this change in assignment came the news that the Combat

Command was attached to the 87th Infantry Division to spearhead them to their objective. The leading elements in the attack advanced with rapidity and early success, but the remainder of the Task Force had considerable trouble with mud before they finally assembled at Kalmuhten. At this point the orders were again juggled around a bit and it became necessary for the Combat Command to return to Dunnwald.

METTMAN

The new mission was to seize bridges on the Dunn and Wupper Rivers and crush the enemy in Opladen. Then Combat Command B was to cross the Wupper and attack toward Mettman to the North. In anticipation of many road blocks, supporting 603rd Tank Destroyers with 90mm guns, were placed well forward in the Tank Task Force which was to lead the attack. The plan proved very worthy, as many road blocks were encountered, and the Tank Destroyers effectively destroyed them, allowing the tanks to proceed rapidly to the Dunn River and seize two bridges intact for crossing. One of the bridges was found to be prepared for demolition by the retreating Germans but was no problem to the expert demolition crew of the first platoon of the Engineer Company. As soon as it was cleared the armor rolled on, deeper into the Ruhr towards the Wupper River

Major General John Wogan

and Opladen. Armored Infantrymen from A and B Companies of the 59th successfully attacked and cleared Opladen of two superior forces of Germans stopping short of the Wupper River. While observing a bridging operation across the Wupper, General Wogan was hit in the neck and shoulder by enemy sniper fire. The command of the division was taken over by Major General John Milliken.

Major General John Milliken.

OPLADEN

The Tank Task Force passed through Opladen on 16 April and found the opposition consisted mostly of road blocks. As the Task Force rolled on toward Haan, one Company C and two Company B tanks fell to antitank guns short of Gruiten. By 1730 hours we reached Mettman and were welcomed by wildly cheering liberated factory workers. The great increase in the number of prisoners taken was beginning to become a problem. A continuous line of Nazi soldiers, with their hands held behind their heads, were marching to the rear.

**German POWs**

DUISBERG
**End of the Battle for the Ruhr**

Units of the Infantry Task Force, C Company of the 59th and A Company of the 24th Tank Battalion (Jack Pyatt's unit) were detached for a special mission under command of G-2, XVIII Corps (Airborne). The remainder of the Task Force plus the Tank Task Force moved in continuation of the attack, meeting no enemy opposition in route. By noon on the 17 April the Combat Command had arrived in the vicinity of Spendeck - Efferscheidt. After which an unopposed march, except for one last concentration of 88mm fire which fell on the column of the 496th as they rode down what was to become known as '88 Alley', was completed in six hours to Duisburg. Driving onward for 24 miles the next day, the 24th Battalion linked with the 17th Airborne Division in Duisberg thus completing on the 18 April 1945, the Battle for the Ruhr. At this point the cessation of all resistance in the Ruhr Valley was announced.

The 13th Armored was still destined to fight under the command of General GEORGE S. PATTON JR., in the Third U.S. Army. On 18 April an order was received returning the division from the First U. S. Army to the rugged Third. Now attached to the XX Corps, the Combat Command departed from the battered and bombed Duisburg and marched to their new assembly area in the vicinity of Siegburg and Gummersbach.

**"Old Blood and Guts"**

After the long march back to the vicinity from which the Ruhr Battle had begun, all units found it necessary to center their attention on vehicular and personal maintenance for a day or two. Along the way, Pyatt recalls, "A Company of the 24$^{th}$ liberated some large chickens they found along the way. They decided to have a hot meal and started cooking the chickens on the exhaust manifold of one of the Sherman tanks. It smelled pretty good until it was served. It was so dry it was not edible. The next time, they boiled the chickens in a pot on the manifold. It was better, but tasted like engine exhaust. It was back to C and K rations after that."

**General Patton of Third Army**

In compliance with orders received by the Division on 20 April, the Combat Command launched out on a two-hundred-and-fifty-mile road march across Southern Germany to the vicinity of Nurnberg, birthplace or Nazism, close to the Austrian border. Due to the long distance of the march an eight hour lay-over in route for chow, rest and maintenance was held at Hanau on 21

April. By late afternoon the next day all units of Combat Command B had closed in assembly areas Southeast of Bamberg. The three-day stay in this position was highlighted by an address by General PATTON to the officers and non-coms of the Division in which he told the Black Cats what was expected of a soldier and an Armored Division in the Third Army.

# AUSTRIA

LINZ

Late in the afternoon of 25 April the Combat Command moved to a forward assembly area and established a Command Post in See, Germany. The new mission for the 13th Armored Division was announced to the officers and men. It was to cross the Danube River and drive directly to the East to make contact with the Russians in the vicinity of Linz, Austria.

**Welcome to Austria**

Both Task Forces sent reconnaissance parties to check on feasible routes and bridges on which to cross the Danube River. Bridges built by the 65th and 71st Infantry Divisions near Regensburg were both considered for the crossing. On the 27 April the Combat Command, with the Tank Task Force leading, moved across the Danube on the bridge of the 71st Infantry Division and attacked to the east and southeast. The head of the column after arriving within the lines of the 71$^{st}$ Infantry Division was held up by enemy artillery. With the night falling fast, it was decided to coil for the night. The Tank Task Force bivouacked for the night outside of Pfatter while the Infantry Task Force spent the night in the vicinity of Moosham. The remainder of the Combat Command bivouacked near Geisling.

**Picking Cherries Along the Way**

During the night plans were drawn up for the next morning's attack. The plan was to have the Combat Command attack to the East in two parallel columns with constant air cover by the liaison planes of the Artillery. The Tank Task Force formed the northern column and the Infantry Task Force the southern. The coordinated attack of the task forces started shortly after 0600 on 28 April.

Tankers advanced almost unopposed to enter the town of Rain, early in the morning. Light opposition slowed the advance and so the Artillery was called upon to paste the town, shelling it with several rounds of white phosphorous mingled with the high explosive shells; many buildings in the town were left burning. The advance continued to the towns of Rinkham and Straubing. The former receiving the same treatment as Rain from the 496$^{th}$ and 177$^{th}$ Artillery fire; the latter was not shelled, because it contained large hospitals with over 5,000 patients. On the outskirts of Straubing the attack was held up only momentarily as a tank dozer cleared a road block from the entrance to the city. Only sporadic resistance from some small-arms fire challenged the crushing drive of the 24$^{th}$ Tank Battalion armor.

ALTERHOFFEN

About noon on 28 April the Combat Command encountered enemy mines in the small town of Alterhoffen. This was its first contact with these familiar German weapons, and they were emplaced so as to block the approaches to a bridge. The mine field was quickly and thoroughly cleared, and the advance moved on until it reached the outskirts of Strasskirhen where an enemy Anti-Tank Gun knocked out one medium tank and held up the attack until the gun was put out of action. Just inside Strasskirchen the tankers again ran into a mine field. This time four tanks from Company C were put out of action by

**Jack Pyatt April 1945**

the mines that were spread out across the road. Smoke from a burning building and from enemy smoke pots had hidden the mines from the vision of the tankers.

After a slight reorganization of the Task Force, B Company of the 24th Tank Battalion, with infantry attachments, and a squad of Engineers from B Company of the 124th Armored Engineer Battalion were given the mission of proceeding as rapidly as possible to the Isar River in the area of Plattling and seize intact, the bridge and secure a bridgehead. A similar mission was given to B Troop of the 93rd Cavalry Reconnaissance Squadron and D Company, 24th Tank Battalion. All three forces proceeded ahead at 1600 hours. Air observation reported that a railway bridge across the Isar River had been blown but the highway bridge was still standing. Just as the troops of Tank Task Forces reached the river the enemy demolished that highway bridge.

On the same day, 28 April, the Infantry Task Force launched its attack from Moosham. Hampered by mud and poor roads, the progress was slow, and it became necessary to detour and retrace several times along the route. Spasmodic mortar and small arms fire harassed the progress of the Infantrymen temporarily, near Ober Hartshausang. This resistance was quickly overrun. The advance again was stopped near Dunnhardt by well dug-in infantry along the Kleinelaader River. This resistance eliminated, the Task Force ran into more trouble in the way of muddy roads and high velocity fire. Fire obtained from the 177th Artillery Battalion took in the enemy positions and wiped out the opposition, allowing the Force to continue almost unopposed to Lailling. Prior to reaching Lailling, where the Task Force coiled to spend the night, an enemy airfield was overrun and taken by complete surprise. All planes on the ground were destroyed by fires of the Infantry and Tanks.

**Swamp Crossing**

At 1100 hours on 29 April, under cover of heavy artillery concentration, the doughboys of A and C Companies of the 59th began operations to secure a bridgehead across the Isar River. The artillery laid down a continuous barrage of fire on the positions of the enemy across the river, putting rounds directly into the foxholes of the German infantry and keeping them all down. During most of the crossing the infantry of the 59th had to wade through water up to their waists.

**River Crossing**

The artillery that had been registering on the opposite bank to a depth of 200 yards also attempted to lay down a smoke screen to cover the armored doughboys, but due to the high crosswinds the screen was only partially effective. However, the covering fire on the far banks of the Isar was so thick and so effective both of the infantry Companies were able to complete the crossing in very short time. Shortly after the crossing was completed the enemy formed for a counter attack, but this too, was repelled by artillery and small arms fire. During the firing that day the 496th fired 2,500 rounds of artillery to support the Infantry making the bridgehead and the Engineers who came up to work on pontoon and treadway bridges.

NEU OTTING

### The Inn River

By nightfall of 30 April the 245th Engineer Combat Battalion had completed the bridge construction and the Combat Command was prepared to jump-off across the river and attack to the East then swing South with the mission of seizing bridges over the Inn River in the vicinity of Neu Otting and Marktl. The plan was to attack during the night in complete blackout and roll as rapidly as possible towards the Inn River. This undertaking was something in the way of a record for the books of the Armored Force. It was

**Inn River April 1945**

the first large scale blackout, armored attack. The combat command spearheaded thirty miles during the darkness of night, meeting no resistance of any consequence. As the troops were rolling through the town of Osterhofen, the largest town the column passed through during the night, the German civilians turned on their house lights and cheered the advancing American Troops. Refugees, Russians, Polish, French and others, tried to climb on the vehicles to cheer and praise their American liberators.

**Damaged Inn River Crossing**

At daylight on 1 May, leading elements ran into strong points of enemy resistance near Malgersdorf. Two tanks in the leading elements of the column were knocked out by Panzer-Faust fire and four 88mm guns were sighted on the crest of a hill dominating the entrance to the town. Tanks, managing to encircle the hill, knocked out the four 88mm's after a fierce exchange of fire. In addition the column was harassed by heavy artillery fire and well-placed machine guns. One of the observation planes of the 496th Armored Field Artillery Battalion was badly shot up while trying to adjust fire on a machine gun holding up elements of the column. The observer in this plane suffered two wounds but the pilot was unhurt and brought the plane in to the landing strip.

EGGENFELDEN

The Task Force in the lead of the attack changed directions and continued the attack to the Southeast as far as Falkenburg where it swung back to the West towards Eggenfelden. Just outside of Falkenburg, two of the dreaded 88-mm's fired on the advancing tanks. In a brilliant display of gunnery two tanks fired one round each and knocked out the two 88mm's before they could fire another round.

As the tanks were approaching Eggenfelden, which had received preparation Artillery fire, the Burgermeister came out to meet the rapidly advancing tanks and surrender the town so as not to have it shot up. After a short debate the Burgermeister was mounted on the front of the lead tank and the column rolled unopposed into the town.

**Knocked Out MK VI Royal Tiger Tank**

Personnel of A Company of the 83$^{rd}$ Medics, reconnoitering for a position to set up an evacuation station in Eggenfelden, captured a German SS Major General, along with his mistress, chauffeur and other members of his staff, all in civilian clothing. Information secured revealed that he had charge of all the concentration camps in this area.

Just South of Eggenfelden D Company of the 24$^{th}$ with attachments of infantry and reconnaissance troops moved by another road to proceed with all possible speed to the Inn River to seize the bridge in the vicinity of Marktl. In the fighting this force encountered in clearing road blocks in route D Company had two Company commanders wounded within two hours. When the resistance became too strong the force withdrew to rejoin the Tank Task Force on the main axis of advance, but was later re-committed to the task of seizing the bridge at Marktl.

The Tank Task Force proceeded to the town of Eisenfelden. As the leading elements placed fire on the approaches to the Neu Otting bridge, it was blown by German demolitions just as B Company, leading the main body reached the bridge. Operations were halted, and the European war ended a few days later. The Combat Command at this point had rolled victoriously over 60 miles in less than twenty-four hours, thirty of which was clicked off in blackout. Troops of B Company of the 59th, aided by Engineers of the 124th crossed the river and occupied most of Neu Otting.

Settling down to garrison life in the picturesque town of Neu Otting, the 24th Tank Battalion cleaned up, rested, played ball, decorated its heroes with 4 silver stars, 69 bronze stars, and 100 purple hearts.

**Bronze Star Award Ceremony**

**2LT Pyatt, CPT Streitle, 1LT Krall**

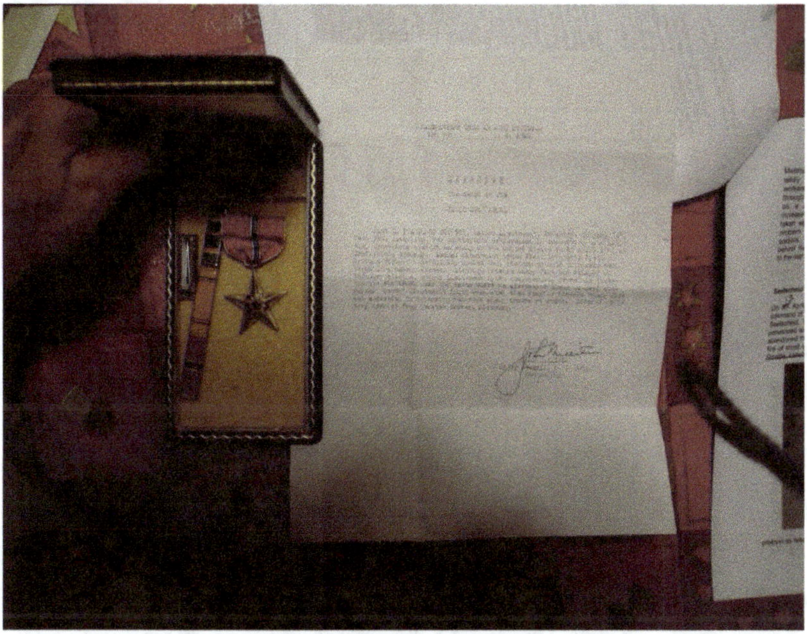

Jack Pyatt's Bronze Star and Citation from Major General Millikin

A few lucky ones drew passes to Paris, the Riviera, and other resort centers while awaiting news about going home. Four battle-tested sergeants, Jarvis, Pyatt, Turnbull and Myers turned in their stripes for new second lieutenant bars.

"On 25 June we boarded our German train for Camp Atlanta, France, near Mailly, arriving there 27 June. Here we crated and packed for the ocean voyage home, took short trips to Paris and Reims and finally entrained 9 July for the staging area in Camp Old Gold. On 14 July we moved by truck to Le Havre, double-loaded on the USS General McRae and steamed for the States. Hampton Roads, Virginia, on 23 July and Camp Patrick Henry for a special dinner—ice cream, milk, fresh fruits and vegetables and steaks. "

**Boarding the USS General J. H. McRae (AP-149)**

By 25 July, the 13th Armored Division troopers were on their way to reception stations then for 30 days back home to rest and get ready for the next round of warfare in the Pacific. Jack went home on furlough to Webster Groves, Missouri and was out squirrel hunting with his brother when he got the word that World War II was over. Filtering back to Camp Cooke, California, early in September, the 13th Armored Division settled down to training, discharges for some and long furloughs for others. Relieved of the task of tackling Honshu, the outfit prepared to end more than two years of eventful service with deactivation late in October 1945.

## EPILOGUE

Jack left the US ARMY and returned to civilian life in St. Louis, Missouri. There in 1949 he met Miss Marion Elliott, a model and freelance photographer from the East Coast. They were married in 1950. In 1962 Jack acquired the White Motor Works unit in Springfield, Missouri. He and Marion moved to Springfield and started their family which would consist of a daughter, Kelly, who still lives in the area and paid visits to Jack and Marion every week end. Marion Pyatt passed away in 2005.

**Marion Pyatt**

## Jack Conrad Pyatt Obituary

Jack Conrad Pyatt, 92, beloved father and grandfather left this world to be with his Father in Heaven, Christ and loved ones that have gone on before, April 1, 2011. He was a man of great love and integrity, and we will miss him terribly.

He was preceded in death by his loving wife, Marion; parents, Harry and Lena; brother, Sherwood; and sister, Lillian. Those he leaves behind on earth are his daughter, Kelly Pyatt Hull; son-in-law Wes Hull; grandchildren, Victoria and Sean; and many dear friends and extended family.

A memorial service was held on Monday, April 4, 2011 at 7 p.m., in the Walnut Lawn Funeral home. Burial took place Tuesday, April 5, 2011 in the Missouri Veteran's cemetery, Springfield, Missouri.

Jack's personal motto was always "Please the People". In his case, we would all agree that the People of the United States of America could not be any more pleased. Jack, thank you for your service.

## ABOUT THE AUTHOR

Martin Capages, Jr. was born in 1944 at Fort Sill, Oklahoma, the son of Marine captain, Martin Capages of NYC and Helen Elizabeth Powell Capages of Millington, Tennessee. As a Marine "brat", he attended elementary schools all over the US along with his three younger sisters. When his parents settled in Missouri in 1956, he attended Dora junior high school and Dora High School in 1958. The family moved to Springfield, Missouri in early 1959 and Martin attended Parkview High School where he was an honor student graduating in 1962. He attended Missouri State University on a Regent's scholarship until 1964 when he transferred to Missouri Science and Technology in Rolla, Missouri, where he graduated in January 1967 with a BS in Mechanical Engineering. At Rolla, he was a Resident Assistant, Distinguished Military Student and Cadet Commander of the Army ROTC Brigade.

After receiving his Commission as an Army Ordnance Officer but prior to reporting for active duty, he joined Boeing Aircraft in Wichita as an Associate Engineer working on the new 737. He reported for active duty in June 1967. Military service during the Vietnam era took him to Aberdeen Maryland, Redstone Arsenal, Fort Knox, and southern Japan where he served as the Officer in Charge of the Kawakami Ammunition Storage area just outside Hiroshima, Japan. While at Fort Knox, 1LT Capages proudly wore the triangular shoulder patch of the US Army Armor Center.

After completing active duty, Martin joined Exxon in Houston, Texas, with assignments throughout the U.S. and Europe. He left Exxon in 1984 to join Kerr McGee in Oklahoma as Manager of Engineering until 1992 when he left the petroleum industry to start his own professional structural engineering consulting firm in Springfield, Missouri. He continued post-graduate studies in Civil Engineering and Management receiving an earned Doctorate in Engineering Management in 2002. He retired from full time practice in 2012. Martin wrote the biography of Jack Pyatt in 2008 and began writing political commentary in 2009. In 2017 he authored *The Moral Case for American Freedom*.

Martin is married to Pamela Kay Capages. They have five children and seven grandchildren. Both Martin and Pamela are active in their Church other international Christian ministries.

## REFERENCES

8th Armored Division. (n.d.). Retrieved from www.8th-armored.org/division/8history.htm.

13th Armored Division, 24th Tank Battalion. (1946). *The 24th Tank Battalion, 13th Armored Division.* Baton Rouge LA: The Army & Navy Publishing Compny, Inc.

Bellamy, P. (2008). *www.13tharmoreddivision.org/497th Armored Field Artillery Battalion.* Retrieved from www.13tharmoreddivision.org.

Bellamy, P. (2008). *www.13tharmoreddivision.org/CCB.* Retrieved from www.13tharmoreddivision.org.

Capages, M. (2008). *www.13tharmoreddivision.org/publications.* Retrieved from www.13tharmoreddivision.org.

Second Calvary Division. (1941). *Historical and Pictorial Review-Second Calvary Divison-Third Field Artillery Battalion.* Baton Rouge LA: The Army & Navy Publishing Company Inc.

# INDEX

12th Armored Division, 10
13th Armored Division, iv, v, x, 6, 7, 10, 15, 16, 17, 34, 45
24th Tank Battalion, 10, 13, 31, 37, 43
4th Armored Division, 16
88, 20, 32, 41
8th Armored Division, 5, 6
Airborne, 17, 31
Autobahn, 19
Bellencombre, 13
Black Cats, iv, 7, 33
blitzkrieg, 4
**BRONZE STAR**, 26
Camp Beale, 6, 7, 9
Camp Bowie, 9, 10
**CAMP BOWIE**, 9
Camp Cooke, 45
Camp Funston, 1
Camp Kilmer, 11
**CAMP KILMER**, 11
Cantley, 27
Combat Command 'A', 15
Combat Command 'B', 13, 15, 16
D-day, 12
Dunnwald, 18, 20, 21, 24, 26, 29
Engineers, 37, 39, 42
English Channel, 12
Exceller, 11
Exxon, 49
First Army, 17, 18
**FORT KNOX**, 5
Fort Riley, 1, 4
**FRANCE**, 13
General McNair, 10

H.M.S. 'Nelson', 12
Headquarters Company, 13, 21
Infantry Task Force, 18, 20, 22, 25, 31, 34, 37
**Inn**, 39, 40, 42
Isar River, 37, 38
Krall, 26, 28
Le Havre, 13, 45
**LE HAVRE**, 13
Marion, 46, 47
Milliken, 30
Missouri, iii, viii, 1, 45, 46, 47, 48, 49
Nazi, 31
Nurnberg, 33
panzerfaust, 25, 26
Panzerfaust, 28
PATTON, 32, 33
Ruhr, 17, 18, 30, 31, 32
Ruhr Valley, 17, 18, 32
Russians, 24, 34, 40
Sea Quail, 11
Second Calvary Division, iv, 1
Seelscheid, 26
Sergeant Pyatt, 5, 11, 13, 27
**Sieg River**, 17, 18, 19
Siegfried Line, 10
Southampton, 12
Springfield, iii, 46, 47, 48, 49
St. Goar, 17
Tank Task Force, 18, 20, 22, 29, 30, 31, 34, 42
Third Army, 33
Tom Thumb, 2
USS General McRae, 45
Wogan, 30
XX Corps, 17, 32

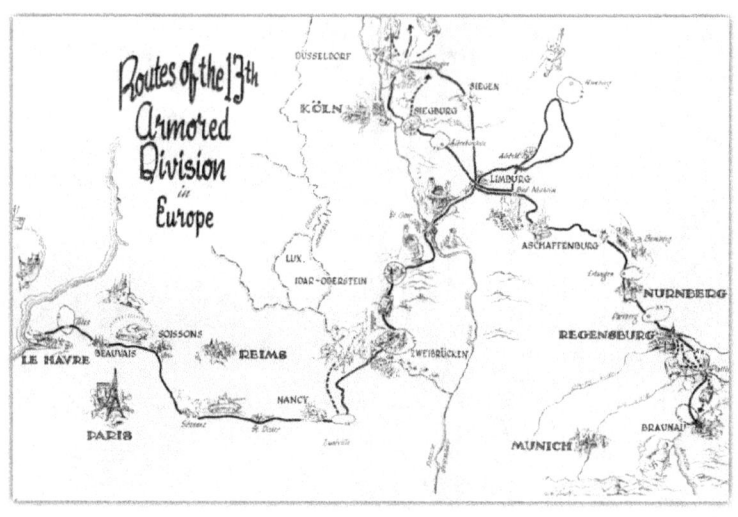

Map Courtesy of the 13th Armored Division

www.ingramcontent.com/pod-product-compliance
Lightning Source LLC
LaVergne TN
LVHW021944060526
838200LV00042B/1921